IT'S TIME TO LEARN ABOUT CANARIES

It's Time to Learn about Canaries

Walter the Educator

Silent King Books
A WhichHead Entertainment Imprint

Copyright © 2025 by Walter the Educator

All rights reserved. No part of this book may be reproduced in any manner whatsoever without written per- mission except in the case of brief quotations embodied in critical articles and reviews.

First Printing, 2024

Disclaimer

This book is a literary work; the story is not about specific persons, locations, situations, and/or circumstances unless mentioned in a historical context. Any resemblance to real persons, locations, situations, and/or circumstances is coincidental. This book is for entertainment and informational purposes only. The author and publisher offer this information without warranties expressed or implied. No matter the grounds, neither the author nor the publisher will be accountable for any losses, injuries, or other damages caused by the reader's use of this book. The use of this book acknowledges an understanding and acceptance of this disclaimer.

It's Time to Learn about Canaries is a collectible early learning book by Walter the Educator suitable for all ages belonging to Walter the Educator's Time to Eat Book Series. Collect more books at WaltertheEducator.com

USE THE EXTRA SPACE TO TAKE NOTES AND DOCUMENT YOUR MEMORIES

CANARIES

High in the trees, so bright and small,

It's Time to Learn about
Canaries

A tiny bird begins to call.

With feathers yellow, like the sun,

The canary sings, a song begun!

Its voice is sweet, so light and clear,

A melody for all to hear.

It chirps and trills, both day and night,

A songbird full of pure delight.

Canaries love to hop and play,

In cages bright or skies so gray.

They flutter wings and stretch up high,

Then soar beneath the open sky.

Their favorite meals are seeds and grain,

With fruits and greens to keep them sane.

A sip of water, cool and sweet,

Makes their little song complete!

It's Time to Learn about
Canaries

In forests wild or homes so neat,

Canaries make a tune so sweet.

A pet so small, but full of cheer,

Their joyful songs bring love so near.

Some canaries shine so bright,

While others glow in hues of white.

Orange, red, and even green,

Their colors make a lovely scene!

Long ago, in mines so deep,

Canaries helped the workers keep.

If air was bad, they'd stop their song,

And warn the men to move along!

Now they live in homes so wide,

With perches tall and room inside.

They love to chirp, they love to play,

It's Time to Learn about
Canaries

And sing a tune throughout the day.

If you see one, watch it well,

It has a tale it longs to tell.

A story sung both bright and free,

A gift of nature's melody!

So listen close, and you will hear,

The canary's tune so bright and clear.

A tiny bird, so bold and true,

It's Time to Learn about
Canaries

That sings a song just for you!

ABOUT THE CREATOR

Walter the Educator is one of the pseudonyms for Walter Anderson. Formally educated in Chemistry, Business, and Education, he is an educator, an author, a diverse entrepreneur, and he is the son of a disabled war veteran. "Walter the Educator" shares his time between educating and creating. He holds interests and owns several creative projects that entertain, enlighten, enhance, and educate, hoping to inspire and motivate you. Follow, find new works, and stay up to date with Walter the Educator™

at WaltertheEducator.com

www.ingramcontent.com/pod-product-compliance
Lightning Source LLC
LaVergne TN
LVHW051919060526
838201LV00060B/4082